# SOUNDING GROUND

# ACKNOWLEDGEMENTS

Some of these poems have appeared in *Bim*, the *PN Review*, *Wasafiri*, *Beyond Sangre Grande*, ed. Cyril Dabydeen, *Caribbean Beat*, *Small Axe*, *POUI*, the *Caribbean Review of Books*.


Highest thanks to the loving, nurturing St. Lucian Literati: Jane King, Kendel Hippolyte, McDonald Dixon, Robert Lee, Travis Weekes et al; to my Trini family: Rawle Gibbons, Nicholas Laughlin, Rhoda Bharath, James Aboud, Giselle Rampaul et al. Immense gratitude to Mark McWatt, Mervyn Morris & Paul Breslin. Thanks to Christian Campbell, Vahni Capildeo and their expansive transatlantic spirits. Special thanks to Tanya Shirley who tongue-lash me to get this collection out & for my brothers and sisters. Highest thanks to all, for your love and the wide caravanserai of your generosity.

VLADIMIR LUCIEN

SOUNDING GROUND

PEEPAL TREE

First published in Great Britain in 2014
Peepal Tree Press Ltd
17 King's Avenue
Leeds LS6 1QS
UK

ISBN 13: 9781845232399

Supported using public funding by
ARTS COUNCIL
ENGLAND

"Essence is a movement. It is the analysis of Ground which tells us exactly what that movement is: Our abstract little spirit who didn't know what he was by his futile becomings was by degrees establishing some Ground." — C.L.R. James

For my father whose work this is a continuation of.
For my mother
For 'Kita & Zion &
for John Robert Lee, my Pòtèz.

# CONTENTS

INTERIOR

COAST

# INTERIOR

# SAMBO I

*for my grandfather, Samuel Lucien*

You would've never think
was the same Sambo who
didn' go no secondary school,
who had to carry the stink
of fish in a basket on his head
walking from Gros Islet to Castries,
the same Sambo who leave
for the war but reach too late,
who eat his farine and fish
in a civilize fight between knife and fork
and etiquette on his plate,
peeling the skin from his avocado pear;
the same Sambo who part his hard hair
like a red sea disagreeing with prophecy,
who spread salvation like a tablecloth
over his soul. Yes, the same Sambo turn
eucharistic minister, justice of the peace.
Who would have known — the way
he carry hisself, the way he have
the presence of a conch-shell blown?

# DONBWÉ

I tell a friend of mine the Kwéyòl word for dumpling
and immediately see my mother's white hands
of flour, that old argument of hands kneading
to claim for themselves a kind of sinking centre,
and I wish I could show her what I mean by *Donbwé*,
show her my mother's hands, the unhurried beating
of a drum, like licks in slow motion –
a measured, thickening pain. I wish I could get
her to overstand the non-dumplingness of *Donbwé*,
the way my mother throws it into a pot of *djòt*,
show her those fingers scribbling seasoning
into food that hands fight wars over.
*Donbwé* is hard, not like the dumpling my friend knows
that yields easy under forks. *Donbwé* demands
immediate teeth, a unique kind of chewing – a meal of labour –
something she may or may not understand;
an argument, perhaps, that must be left to hands.

# MY GRANDMOTHER'S MIND
*For Manman*

Many times what is on my grandmother's mind
is what to cook when she gets home
for her husband, the man's man. We call him
"Pah-pah", like the sound of two quick slaps,
like the sound of the catapult-slippers that
smack his hard foot-bottom when he walks out
with his man's stride out into the field, potbellied
and satisfied like Barbados. My grandmother,
"Ms. Yoolee", carries that thought like a basket
of unsold produce on her head from the market
in Bridgetown, leaving behind the hot memories
of arguments and strife, the damp salad of her worries,
things that – were she to carry them all in her basket –
would weigh her down, would make her not want to cook
for this man's man with his man's stride coming in like an ogre
from hard-working in the field. At the end of the day,
nearing Christ Church, she has always known what to cook.
But more than that she has always known what to burn.

# MEDIUM

*"That we may learn to bear the beams of love…"* — Blake

We never knew the cousins whose deaths
my mother came to announce,
the cousins, she said, that asked for us
all the time, who couldn't pronounce
our "educated" names: *Gladeemeh, Pahblo, Enkooma.*
We just knew that Mummy liked to look for relatives,
to find blood where there was only water.
Deep inside Monchy where they came from
was only mango trees and bush that whispered
like city children when country bookies
got up in school to talk *prupper Ingleesh;*
Monchy, where my mother grew up,
where she would be put on a table with her golden skin,
like a trophy, reading English and Education
in that cousin and cousin-make-dozen world
of close blood. She would return from those funerals
in dark clothes, alone, shaken, with a leaflet
dropping delicately from her hand, letting go
of another relative for us as she took off her bra,
releasing her breasts, loosening her heart
until the next cousin comes, through her, to our house
like a guest, wiping earth from his feet.

# BASIL

The boys still slamming their dominoes
outside of Broda's place. Basil,
who use to be a sweet-boy in his day,
starring in the Country & Western
dances, use to be a carpenter, he say,
with the best wood in the whole island,
now sits limp and old,
slamming dominoes hard
on the table with three of his partners
wearing their crumpled fedoras push back
on their heads. Basil has had 'nough
woman in his day, has drowned his liver
in rum and good company, has lived
all the life he ever cared to live.
Now, he has built a long line of dominoes,
holding the last one in his hand, suspended
over the board, knowing that on either end
of that long, white road with its small black dots,
like a map of all the funerals he has attended,
it is his turn to play; that no matter what
any of his partners do, they cannot stop him; no matter
how much his children-mothers quarrel tonight
a man don't go home until he ready.

# STONE

My great great grandfather from Antigua
taught the locals how to make good-quality cement,
how to turn a forest grey with a few
scoops swooping over the left shoulder,
how to tame the low jungle of pebbles,
sand and lime, how to flatten things
in time. Whole cities splattered
behind him, tossed over the cold shoulder
of unfortunate decades — savannahs of stone
and brick, thick forests of walls, vineyards
of barbed wire, the swift current of promenades.
Nothing swayed in the breeze where he had been,
just cities stiff like straightened Negro hair;
nothing but his shovel making its own wind,
flinging grey waves over his shoulder.
None of the buildings, the cities would ever be his,
but he never looked back long enough to know.
He was content with a shovel, sunlight
weeping in his armpits and a little cement
powdering his body at the end of the day,
hardening his heart, breaking him apart
on the small sidewalk of his dreams.

# THE WORLD OF FLAT THINGS

> "Sentez-vous la douleur d'un homme
> de ne savoir pas de quel nom il s'appelle?
> A quoi son nom l'appelle?"
> — Aimé Césaire, *La tragédie du roi Christophe*

In my father's time everyone had —
along with their grander Christian names —
a name that stretched across the long
shadows of the afternoon, summoning
children from wherever they were
in the savannah. It was called their *non-savann,*
and always had vowels that would befit
a long drawling bellow that could shake
the air's frame but never disrupt
the peace of the homes within it.
Mothers knew that wherever their sons
would roam that name would bring
them back to the makeshift stair,
eager to assist in the most onerous chores
from tying unruly goats
to scrubbing knee-abrading floors.

There were those who went astray occasionally,
who followed a track beyond the savannah of flat things
where no unforeseen future could hide,
where voices begin to break violently in their throats
and pieces of light fall through the trees,
and souls — like an attack of mealy bug —
become spoiled and speckled with sin.
No Christian name ever called those prodigals back
to their mother's stair, to the ropes on goats grown slack,
or floors long unscrubbed. But whether
they came back as murderers or men,
their mothers could call them back again

bellowing that *non-savann* of their boyhood
that stayed the same, though the shadows grew
in the afternoon, and with them they would bring
their round faces back to the predictable world of flat things.

# BUSH TEA

*For Helen*

Your faith has always been
this gathering of leaves,
this beetle of fire lying on its back,
this blossoming flower of boiling water.
Your rituals: the hot movements
within the brightening walls of this house,
your sacred grove of domestic busyness.
The way you boil the morning into being,
boil us up from our dreams
to this miracle of tea, two or more leaves
gathered in our names, a simple kind
of obeah, that makes us rise from the bed.

# A PICTURE

My father use to wear an afro in the '70s –
black champagne on his head – when
he had awaken from the deceptions
of the System, from the sticks and stones
that shatter his reflections, that defile
his ancestors, that hit them; his eyes
averted from the dark-dark Ages,
from the bad breath of History yellow
pages. My father come from a good home –
his mother does pray the decades
of the rosary and his father does carry a brief case –
a place where they still have a picture
of him from back then, black and white and torn,
something the years had worn
and forgotten, sitting there with his drum
between his legs: conscious, awakened,
his senses sharpened, nose spread out
on his face like it asking,
**"W    h   a' p   p   e   n?"**

# ITAL

*for Nkrumah, brother, & Mokocho*

From time to time I eat at an ital shop
in a cramped corner of town. It has been
here for years – rickety, ramshackle pieces
of wood bunched together like the thick
crunch of locks on the rastaman's head
under the smothered ambition of his tam.
In this storm of concrete that has
come to this town, that has stolen the identity
of ground – snidewalks that slide under our lives,
the nice-nice escalator that steals our
footsteps and walks calmly ahead of us,
the seriousness of cement, the sweet hum
of car and truck and van –
I come to this bold breakable icon,
standing zemi-faced, the i-and-i of the storm,
this shack where I come to the warm
welcome of food that does not taste
of haste or hustle, that does not taste
of dungle. And so I & I path through this jungle
of greens, through this white ixora of rice
through secret societies of spice
that does not leave the smell of flesh
or blood on my breath and, as Priestman say,
does not taste of death.

# THE LAST SIGN OF THE CROSS

My brother left the Church
with his final sign of the cross
of forehead sweat, tie pin
and shoulder pads of jacket,
when the worshippers kissed
white Mary's statue.
My mother laments
that her little boy into whose chest
she rubbed dry oaths
of Vick's Vapour rub
has abandoned God,
the little boy whom she
baptized in the name of
  the Father
   a n d
  of the Son
who is seated at the right hand
of God, hunched like a faucet
waiting to wash away our sins.
She is sorry that her little boy
cannot accept the Holy Spirit.
But he has left, walked out
of the church with its rust, its stone,
its dust, walked beyond his mother's caul
of worry in search of a place
that tells his story, touching his shoulders
with his final sign of the cross,
the Holy spirit jockey backing on him
like a *lwa*, a child, an albatross.

# THE STORY OF TOUTOUNI

Feeling that they were without sin,
three men took off their clothes and,
as though they had heard the roll called
up yonder, thundered out of the world,
shouting "FIRE! FIRE! FIRE!"
But nothing burned. Everything remained
as it had been. Up in the hills, feeling now
that they were related to sky, that they
had ceased to desire the World, they listened
without guilt to the sweet songs of birds,
the pure and mellow melodies of bees;
they asked permission of plants to pick their leaves
and flowers. In their nakedness they spent
undiscriminating hours meditating on the body –
their sleeping skin dribbling sweat; their perfectly
brown bowel movements; measuring manhood
in the foam of their piss. They tied the beauty
of the world to their hearts; saw things borning and dying,
watched themselves bleeding and healing; watched from night
to morning leaves gesturing, grass whispering, snakes
hissing; they watched things ferment in the light
of the sun. Then one dry season, one of them stood up,
with locks of ideas tangled inside his head, broke his meditation
into three pieces, gave it to his disciples and said:
*What about feeling we rights like roots firm in this soil?*
*What about di Equal Rights of tings dat be an' continue to is?*
*What about Di Divine Right of Tings?* And they held still
at the top of that hill, sitting so lightly on the ground,
scrolled their wisdom around the herb of truth,
and passed the burning bush around.

## OVERSEER: GOOD HAIR

We learned to hide from the Boss who
walked in the tick-tock of his shoes,
shimmering & clocking down the hall, counting down
to trouble and detention for our trespasses.
Confiscator of chains, rubber wristbands,
chokers; grand inquisitor for practical jokers,
hooligans, belligerents and perverts.
In third form, afros rose like the walls of
some medieval city, a rampart against the Boss's
reign. He had them all chopped down, blew
them off our heads with threats, snapping at each
defiant tuft of *nèg*, watching them fall like smoke
wafting toward the ground. In fourth form
we discovered the slick-back and spent
hours in the mirror, concerned, foppish,
our ancestors Percy Sledge, Smokey Robinson
and the Temptations. We tiptoed through the halls
our hair packed with grease, gel, cold press
– anything that would make our hair
lie down and behave and shine like the Boss's
shoes. With our hair quiet for so long,
our feet graceful tiptoeing around the school,
Boss became suspicious, glancing askance
at us; spent Monday assemblies
contemplating how he could wheel
and come back again. One day, walking the halls,
my hair resisting the grease, wriggling
in the sticky grasp of gel, shaking in the wind
like an *annafè* girl, the boss swooped round a corner,
grinning like a little boy who has caught a lizard.
He spun me around, shouting my last name, his mouth
spread wide with hide-and-seek glee, made
swiftly for my head and pulled my hair free.

# OVERSEER: DETENTION

The afternoons grew more humid
on Thursdays when there was detention,
boys gathered in a room, unsettlingly quiet,
half-asleep, making jets with homework
papers – the teacher as bored as the students.
Sometimes, the Boss hosted "repeat offenders"
in a Detention Special, and we lined up
with rags, gloves and rubbing-alcohol,
were marshalled about the school, rubbing
out our cannon of graffiti, bursting out laughing
when we came across drawings
of penises, our mothers' breasts or the
one heroic epigram saying, "Boss, bullar".
We sprayed and wiped off our names, losing
ourselves in the fumes of the alcohol.
Boss carried a half-smile the whole
time. You could always catch him
doing this – smiling from somewhere deep
inside him, as if from knowing that
every crop of boys will find a way
to disturb the walls of his authority,
and he will punish them like budding Mau Mau,
*nèg mawon*. He wanted to be here
for all of it, all the repeating shapes
of that lifelong game, where the more things changed
was the more they stayed the same.

## OVERSEER: RANKS

The school went up in arms and uproar
like a protest in one of them
Middle-East countries you does see on TV,
when Ranks gave the Boss a *gòjèt*,
caught him with a hook-handed jab to the throat.
Nobody went to class that day,
a six-hour long period of lessons
in mayhem and revolt. Boys breathed
fire on the whole plantation of postures,
pointing our finger-guns to the skies
as teachers stood outside the staffroom
in shock and indignation, burning.
It must've started that day
when his mother came in second form
to beat Ranks in front of the Boss,
to show – like parents used to do
to please priests in the old days –
her total intolerance of upsetting the way
things were and forever should be.
From then Ranks revolted, cursed teachers,
wagged his tongue at the Boss, waved
his middle finger at the Virgin Mary statue –
on her Saint's day. But after that massa-day-done
when he became our Patron Saint of Resistance,
Ranks rolled and rolled and gathered no moss.
He dropped out, smoked himself
to madness, dressed in rags. The teachers invoked him,
reduced to his Christian name "Ethelbert",
to show us – what lesson exactly?
Ranks was a good boy when he first came.
Neat, school shoes polished,
the seam in his pants slicing wind
as he walked. He said nothing in class,
talked only when spoken to. Nobody

26

tells that part of his story now, the whole
tale broken and bent over like a boy being caned.
When we saw him in the street, you could tell
he was no longer himself, no longer with us,
grown *mèg,* a kind of afterlife.
He was our lesson, too, a flint-rock
sparking one fiery memory
of that glory day, that attempted coup
when our school became the Middle East,
nearly Biblical, when Ethelbert
aka Ranks, almost, almost slayed the Beast.

## OVERSEER: EPILOGUE

And so the Boss, who we knew had
loved us, let us go the only way he knew how,
from the black and white uniforms into
those that he'd worn for decades
of college boys — shirt sleeves, soft-pants, shiny
shoes. Then he waits for the fresh, new,
bald-headed crop, green and round-faced
like calabashes, clattering into the schoolyard,
excited about being the cream,
about long-held Traditions,
a new crop that he must season,
nurture and cane. Every year,
he must sit at his desk and ponder,
at pains to remember time in five year periods,
wondering what makes now
different from then? What new world
will issue from these indifferent hands?
He climbs the stairs, comports
himself before the rostrum and from far inside
the world of forms and prefects & competitions,
fights & unseen reconciliations, detentions & punishments,
observes the orbit of boys around him,
and gives a speech not too different from the one last
year or the year before,
repeating each time with more conviction,
his plea for this year to change it.

# BLACK LIGHT

*Re-membering Walter Rodney*

It inevitable that all o' we bound
to step on our shadow foot
and not say sorry, that our mothers
can only teach us what manners
was when she was small, and worry
about if we will be good people,
if we will say thank you and please,
that we would ask and receive, that
the hard times go ease up,
that nobody can buckle our knees
and tell us we hungry, and there will always be
light in our eyes and bread in our hearts.
But is because you start givin' the system backchat,
tellin' too much to the bredren and sistren,
bringing down the bar-graph of Babylon buildings,
measuring underdevelopment, grounding
downpressers to dust, demanding
bigger manners like freedom, equal rights & justice –
permission to be your skin and yourself, please!
Is because you did not hold your peace in your pants'
pocket, did not take your UWI cheque quiet
with it signature hissing fast like a snitch, that the light
switch on you with a rage, willing to blow out the candle
that you was, your afro blazing from your scalp, down there
in Burnham gold-tooth El Dorado. And to think
that in Georgetown, in Kingston, and down
in Bridgetown, youths with good heads on their shoulders,
Vaseline shining on their foreheads like futures, white
powder on their chests keeping their hearts cool,
will go to school and learn all kind of nothing
about themself, that they will mash their shadow foot
as it go behind them. How one day, one of them,
one of your own, playin' smart, go deny you, go spit
their new light on the darkness of your heart.

## AT THE GRAVE OF C.L.R. JAMES

The epitaph is slightly faded
as though the rains had stopped
for a moment inside his name and cried
not knowing who he was, but that there
was death here and that it was strong.
The name is fading on the grave
of a man who would have held the rain
of the world here inside each solitary
letter, who would borrow a firm silence
from epitaph just to listen, not only to its falling
or its close associations with dirt and madness,
but the rising sound of heavy showers, the thunder
of its hunger, its relationship by blood to morning
by way of dew. He, more than any of us, knew
how to talk to the rain as equals.

# THE TRUE SOUNDS OF NUMBERS

I want to hear the true sound of numbers,
the startling statistics of AIDS victims,
diabetes per capita, genocides, holocausts,
numbers of mumbling slaves packed together
in the hold. I want to hear fists hiding fingers
like Jews from Einsatzgruppen. I want a pie-chart
for a heart, apportioned by racial demographics.
I want to count leaves of cane. I want to count fire –
multiply it by what it manages to burn to ash. I
want to count bodies unaccounted for. I want
to know the population of all the world's absences.

In the churches there are people singing
at funerals, dressed in the colour of numbers,
singing about death and separation to a decimal place.
I want to paint murals of numerals,
to trace a long division sum of time back to the beginning,
to find again the true sound of numbers.
I want to hear in these congregations of silences,
this world of disease, of people needing organs,
the sound of numbers, whether they bleat,
or weep, or sing like birds. Or does the true
sound of numbers come from things
for which we do not have the words?

# TJENBWA: NEOPHYTE
### for R., W., W., B., O

*"Force whatever its morality, has its function and merit*
*and must be recalled (theatred) and placed at man's disposal"*
— Rawle Gibbons

*"What did men live by? What did they want? What did history show that they*
*had wanted? Had they wanted then what they wanted now? The men I had*
*known, what had they wanted?"*
— C.L.R. James, *Beyond a Boundary*

An old black pot
is propped on an old wheel
in the yard, where a small
fire is burning. A man rises
slowly from the sodden
secret of his bedding. Last
night at the crossroads, he
and the Devil old-talked and
slammed dark dark dominos;
pawned his pulse for the fleck
and flow of tarot cards.
Today, rainflies insist on a particular
piece of air where something is turning
or has turned.

# TJENBWA: NIGHT-SHIFT

Some nights he does turn into a pig, a black cat.
Some nights he does squawk his own name
from the lungs of a *malfini*. Some nights
he does undress from his skin, flying out as a flame
to see how the night would unfold. And
when his son had get big enough, when the boy
pee finally start to make bold foam in the dirt,
he teach him how to be something more than a man,
teach him the art of transcending his balls, how to wear
the legs of cows under his skirt, to be deep and dark
and unanswerable, like the pit-toilet he was now above,
chanting down his poverty with something like wings.
Every night now, going out to work obeah –
making something of himself.

## TJENBWA: PROTEAN

The moth that enters
your house at night is a grudge
that somebody is holding
against you. It half-sits, bothered
by your light and the roof
over your head. It spreads
its small evening wherever
it lands over the things
you love most. A dark tent
of dark intentions.

# TJENBWA: KÒKMA

*Numen inest — There is a spirit here*
— Ovid, *Fastii*

Something... there
while you sleeping, something
that does come over you sudden-sudden
and hold you tighter than skin, cold
like night-time window sill
something still... there... holding you
as if from within.

They say the cure for *Kòkma*,
when it hold you in the night,
is to throw your head back
like a bride's bouquet and calmly
say, over and over, the Hail Mary
and Our Father, to gather them
like beads on your tongue,
a quick rosary of spit, scapular
of tongue and chant...
chant loud as dreams until it drop you.


And if the *Kòkma* don't let go,
if you still feel this naked feeling
like something wrap your own skin
tight round your bones, if that feeling don't go,
if, after you pray, you still feeling so:
close your eyes to the light.
Don't fuss nor fight.
Tonight, the world
in all its indifference felt that you
needed to be held.

## TJENBWA: GWAN BWA

VL: Why does it do that?
R: Because of the spirit.
VL: Why does the spirit make that noise?
R: That is the kind of tree it is. That is how it is.
Once is twelve o'clock it have to whinny.

And there are eyes that see
this belief system of branches,
ears that hear the soft voices of fruit
and find their humility
in small unassuming seeds;
eyes that see birds
that will eat the small insects
of your sins on the backs
of cows, how the whole world
culminates in an afterlife
of roots. Here, somewhere
near the dark pond that dons
its hats of water lilies, past
the *pawasòl djab*, a plant
waits in the patience of
its stem for the man who
will pay it to use its leaf
to cure those who have been
left suffering, with rosaries
dangling like lianas upon
the tree of Man, waits
for the man who is walking towards
midday when the shadow switches
sides and the day takes the left-
handed path to dusk;
where at midday the *bwa demou*
must shake and proclaim
its belief in the Devil.

# TJENBWA: DEVIL'S BRIDGE, MORNE LEZARD

*for Vahni Capildeo*

Now, you concoct your own geography:
to roads that should have shrivelled
into primitive paths of red dirt,
that should've stained your shoes,
led you to the squat satisfaction
of some zinc-roofed hut.
You should've felt the loneliness
of all the night's windowsills, the fleeting
interest of a small rain – signs and tunnels
that disallow your height. Everywhere
there is this wilderness of maps
that will show you things:
rivers that can fit beneath fingernails;
coasts where water is afraid; boundaries
too thin to police until a map starts to grow
from the seeds in its soil, and trees and places
push past their Christian names,
and an island discovers its wet, riverine spine.
And having crossed your bridge, adventurer,
pioneer, you must stumble now
upon the scattered heartbeat of potholes,
your raised, wayward conscience.

# TJENBWA: SACRIFICE

*"During my researches in the British Museum, I came across a pamphlet of thirty pages entitled 'The Monchy Murder: The Strangling and Mutilation of a Boy for Purposes of Obeah.' It is a sordid story. The boy, Rupert Mapp, twelve years of age, had been enticed away from Bridgetown, Barbados… A week later his body was dug up but it was found that the two hands, and the heart had been removed.* – Father Joseph J. Williams

*VL: What do the spirits want from man?*
*RO: If you have the spirit working for you,*
*you have to feed the spirit. It's just like your*
*son or your daughter – working for you. You have to feed it.*

We don't know

nothing about Obeah

but we want to know

how somebody could

inflict all that wickedness

and pain on hearts that

does beat so delicate

so fast like puddles

under rain

# TJENBWA: ETHNOGRAPHY

You have come with your recorder,
pens and notebook in your satchel,
to find again these old men who laughed
like dominoes mixing your childhood
on a shaky wooden table, to find the women
who moved about them gently, like smoke
from their cigarettes, who left trays
of fruit outside their homes, awaiting
the soft wrath of rot or the rare buyer –
women, so tired of leaving things
to God, or the man who forgets everything
for the rum shop; never too down in the mud
to drink Jesus blood, never too dead with tired
to eat from his bread, but there are things
that can be done out of sight, there are ways.
You ask them about the dark practice, whispering
your question like bush. The answers
dangle over you like fruit, daring you
to climb the dark bark of the tree
if you want the truth.

# CENTIPEDE

When we first discovered the new place
we hung clothes like flags in the closets –
I building a rampart of books, she hanging
curtains, a hammock, erecting framed photographs
like decoys in every nook and cranny.
Everything was new and clean and perfect
until that centipede came hundreding
into our lives, invading our space,
a low, one-man army creeping, advancing
on elbows. But we struck definite blows:
hurling shoe-grenades, wielding brooms,
capsizing furniture – throwing our whole life
at the thing. It ducked and hid somewhere, laid low
so that we never found it. We spent that whole night
on the bed with the lights on, petrified of falling
asleep, the whole house unsettled and strange.
We wanted closure, to find it curled in a corner
dying or dead, but the floors seemed to fall deeper
the further you were from the bed.

# HOME

Home is where
when the public
world is dark
we turn on
a private
light.

# HORN

*Water*

It's like the foam of the sea at the mouth
of my door, like Moruga beach menacing over
my Welcome mat, ready to drown family and future
and the small windows of bills with our names together
and our exact place on earth from where we will look
out beyond the big navel of the electric meter
and we will say "morning"
to the disappearing neighbours of our days
and sit in our firm foundation of furniture
that you rearrange every other evening like
      the warm, turning sea.

*Ice*

But I see myself now opening the soft
sibilance of the freezer door. I open the frost
of secrets of our home to find us bleeding
at the mouth, to find that that fresh flesh
in the secret freezer of my new privacy have us
bleeding, spilling and flowing under empty ice trays.
I close back the freezer and am deaf again, cannot hear
me leaving, cannot see me opening the late door
of our night that we had already closed.
Was like I find I leave the sugar bowl
of your heart open to the ants, small
and gathering like suspicion, like I open
our home, our flesh, in the middle of the night to the wolves…

*Melt*

Now it returns and returns, turns and turns
over like the sea, scattering any chance of dreams,
shattering the smiling cowrie shells of our plans;
it is like Pigeon Island where we does bathe
on Sundays, but on the next side,
without the pressure of tourists, without
the horses and music, but where they have birds,
plenty plenty birds, flying so carefully
so faithfully in the fixed flow of their flocks
and the sea, our sea of things, the rolling accumulation of our times,

gathers itself and breaks your heart over and over again,
bleeding small-small bubbles on the rocks.

# RAINFIGHTS

May we always argue
and suffer the intervention of rain
and thunder that sends us lightning
into each other. We are
overflowing with things to say.

But we bring up bygones, raise
to scrutiny patterns of action
of painful consequence. May we say
nothing and listen to the greater
argument of rain, to the possibility
of lost roofs and landslides outside.
It will subside, and like mud,
we will survive it all.
The tired sky will shine again.

The gutters will dry up
and we will turn over ourselves,
each holding our private
puddle of pain.

# PASTORAL

And love would be a herd of moments grazing
upon memory when we turn back gazing,

and not one of them may ever lift a face
from the pastoral, from that unvaried place

to give us a meagre look, or in lazy mistrust
raise its head, masticating mouthfuls of lust,

pretending recognition, watching you yearn.
Because the past has a way of being polite

that the present has no time to learn,
it will tell you "good morning",

it may tell you "good night",
but no moment will ever speak out of turn.

COAST

## TO CELEBRATE ST. LUCIAN CULTURE
## THEY PUT ON DISPLAY

A chamber pot
an old iron
something
to do with us
indiscernible
with rust

# MI JEAN

You look to the hills
and the impossible
huts of squatter settlements
where children become
the negative elements,
the *zonbi* haunting the streets,
the badjohns who die like toads
with their insides leaping in front them
on the road or, *mesi Bondyé*,
the bright bright sons
who couldn't go university
to learn about Marx and Hegel
and will die not knowing
how to dialectic properly
because there was no
land, no land, not enough last name
to get the loan – the bright bright
son who sets forth alone, early morning,
into the sad leaves of bananas,
the dejected track that trickles
down the slope to the valley
held in the scare-quotes of vultures;
the son who works his way
into the hot land,
into the day's rhythm of goats
and trees and shade and shadows,
must climb and descend
the impossible hill of his heart,
with all his ambitions sinking
into the thick of his calves,
as he grumbles through his life
like a pipe without water,
as he grows away from his books
with the invincible bookmarks

of his chores. All he has now is his mother's
cool arms, his mother who boasts
about her boy, about how long his long
division sums used to be, about how
much language he could talk. The boy,
who used to dream beyond this island
unmannerly with mountains, walks
each day into the small principle of
a swept yard, and waits on
the bubbling pan of his mother's pride
propped on her coalpot of burning black things.

# REDUIT BEACH

Sometimes I grow tired
of the sun, of the hot, armpit-dark
prospects, Mama, of the hired
happiness of them blue beaches,
of being among the leeches;
tired of those Manilla men with
profit tucked in their closed
folding faces;
tired of the stale dreadness of songs,
of this dread heat, of the easy-skankin'
of long hours across the hot, sweatin' day
sellin' seashell chains by the seashell shore,
listenin' to the loud whispers
of transistor radios, men settling scores,
hearin' the blue waves roar.
I can take that long-sleeved breath,
Mama, and work the hours with the shirt-in-pants
no advance pay-cheque. I can close my mouth
over opinions screeching like chalk.
I can cut the dread talk and learn how to peck
past the breadline.
I can meet the deadlines, spit-shine my reality,
lace up my boots.
I can wear the hot suits
and smile and learn how to file
the papers...
But I keep hearing the salt taper
within the slow hours
of the beach's airborne days
and I can't seem to breathe
out them headstrong ways,
so I found me a white girl, Mama,
who don't mind how my hair curl

with eyes white white white
that calm me like the sea-foam.

So when my heart comes knock-knock-knockin',
tell it I'm not home. And here,
where I've gone, sometimes the rain falls
and the strands of God's clear conscience
pile up in the puddles (shows you your own face,
makes you cover your head and know your place.)
Sometimes, Mama, hardly a thing can be seen
when fog hangs in the air like a barber spraying sheen.
Sometimes, so many times, the rain falls
on not-my-sunshine
and I'm too far from me to hear your call.

# DECLARATION
*Description of Articles*

Baron Pepa
tamrin balls
guava jam
guava cheese
lowcal rum
coco stik
fish rap
in nuse paper
sinnerman
nutmeg
spice rum
Bay rum
sof candel
Cocoanut balls
fuj
tablet
seizenings
a whole
dam
ham
a dasheen
a yam,
breadfruit
a hand
of greenfig
mango
long, sweet
mango julie
mango ti fi
a hard flat biscuit
call lababad
name after Bar-

bados, Bull
that the old women
use to make
in they home &
a old time sweet
call comfut

# CRANE

Well, Jimmi get a works wiff a flim
company up in Canayda, an' he usin'
camera and all, not the one dat takin' out picture
but di one in di movies,
doing big tings in dat country
of whitepeople, makin' dem turn
pink wiff jealousy like strawberry
smoothy. He almos' lose me
in all his talk. Girrllll, he even
talkin' funny, as doh he talkin' too much
with people in di company. Talkin'
like he livin' in Canayda for years,
pronouncin' all his R's in his new
accent! Well, he starrrt to talk about
tracks an' cracks an' computer
an' lenses. Girrrrrl, he start to confuse
me. I doh know nuffing about dem tings.
I seein' all di new children, dey souls
fresh like smoke-herring, dey fingers soundin'
like rats running on di keyboards,
an' dey writin' whole sentences in a little bitta letters.
Lord, wha' you go do? Di children mus' grow.
But den Jimmi catch my attention. I tell you,
he amaze me when he tell me about the crane –
is a set of metal bars like a long metal arm
that does lif' di camera high, high, above
di cameraman eye. It does capture all kine of ting:
trees, sky, di whats an' di whys.
*Mwen menm.* I know is different time, different
vision, I know Jimmi is KFC an' I is groun' provision,
but I doh trus' dis crane ting, I doh trus'
all dis television fuss, and all dis crane,
dat taking our vision, an' going high high,
wiff it clear eye into di sky, how all dis takeknowledgy

just above our head, like it doh even need we
again to move forward. Lord, protech my Jimmi
from di world of cranes, dat use
his sight but leave him on di groun'.
Bring my Jimmi away from dat crown
of thorns of dat strange cold sun, from
dose new birds of prey holding our eyes
in dey clause, dat press pause an' play
on our life. Bring his round face safe
from di world of trains and cranes
back home wiff its walking
distance of love, back to our mornings
of reachable roosters. Even doh
he go back to being Rasta, an' smoking
marijuana, even doh he go back to not far-wardin'
metal, an' start his talk about I an' I an' I,
because Lord, excuse my tone,
back den, his eye was his own.

# CIRCLE

In the little circle at lunch time,
the girls' and the boys' mouths chiming
with songs like:
*Pink girls ah pinky dou*
*Pink girls ah djouké sa,*
*ah ya yay ah djouké sa!*
*Oy yo yoy ah djouké sa!*
And boys wining with girls,
girls wining with girls, boy wining
with boy, and Sister Jess, with her panty high
up in her waist, hearing the noise, come out in
the door of her classroom to watch, to see
what is the cause of all them little laughters,
all that snickering like rat feet running in the rafters,
all that happily-ever-after of lunch time.
And she see a circle, and it growing bigger
with children, more and more children,
and Patsy in the middle of the belly of that beast
of a circle like a navel. And she getting on slack!
And they singin:
*My mudda send me to school,*
*to learn my A B C*
*Di teacher call me damn fool,*
*I call her damn fool back!*
And Patsy go straight in front of Sheldon,
and she wine, and she wine and she wine
down to the bottom of Sister Jess' morality,
low,
low,
low,
and Sister Jess seeing all that contact
of flesh put her eyes to the sky, nod her head
back down to reality, then gone in the class.
When she come down the stairs

she spot Patsy with her waist flickering
like a star cast in darkness
and give her seven lash of stick in her ass. WADAPS!
Just like that. Patsy crush up her face
like homework paper, and start bawling
the place down. She throw herself on the ground
and Sister Jess, still hot in her head, with her parachute panty
didn't yet come back down to earth.
She eh even hear Patsy suckin her teeth, choopsin'
loud like nobody business. Sister Jess was tired.
And she couldn't believe is that little thing
that get her tired so. But then days and months passing,
and the circle of her belly gettin' rounder, and she feeling
something getting on inside her, and like her panty
couldn't even cover her navel again. The Priest and
them start to watch her, and she bow her head,
'cause she had know. And before the circle of her belly
could grow, she go to a old doctor
in the clean white secret of his office, and she put a end
to all that "*djanmbélé djanmbélé djouké sa*" in her belly,
to take out the ring-game in there,
and just so, just so, Sister Jess turn she circle
back into a square.

# SAMBO II

Now, Sambo cannot even sign his name,
cannot remember how it use
to spell respectability in a few letters,
and in his frail attempts
you can feel something melt-
ing, like memory or the need for it.
The same Sambo who get a degree
in America, his hand crawling, his handwriting
sprawling like a fall he take in town
in front of everybody. Syllables tripping
on themselves, spiting him, running stupidly
into each other in a dying font.
Is like the English accent has gone
out of his handwriting, like priests suddenly
forgetting their Latin, or his signature's sagging,
cursive fences being invaded
by something outside of himself.
Sambo, who learnt Morse-code in Trinidad,
who wrote home so surely from Guyana, who
spoke the perfect posture of English, reduced
to his bedroom day after day, his hands shaking,
unable to write, like the poor & illiterate of Gros Islet:
he grows away from us in the local way.

# CORBEAU

Corbeau rises
and flaps our world downward,
because the earth comes to terms
with itself first through its birds,
looming above the identities of days,
rubbing shoulders with rain.

Corbeau rises
and lowers our earth to us like bait,
because it is ours, and in his wisdom, quietly,
he waits      he waits      he waits
politely, until we have finished ourselves.

Corbeau rises,
removes himself from the world
or the world from himself,
manoeuvring through the low, difficult blue
until he is all sky. He rises dimly, darkly with
his neck of mail. Shard of night, diving swiftly:
"Prey prey prey!" he says. His business
is what remains.

# DEATH OF A STEEL BASSMAN

We know that your heart
was cake with dirt, and that
when you beat the big drums
the black steel bloom of your bass
was like a big bottom shaking under
the outskirts of Conway, Marchand,
Laventille, and you could hear the music
limping from one note to the other with
your hands like two gunshots stuck in it leg.
Hold your *sigawèt of tabak* in your mouth and play
it like low kind thunder that we can touch,
like something from down under, bassline
so free, so low, bass like a big black shadow of sound,
bass like the deep voice of shade cooling
down our backs. And we hearing it going on
and on, without sleeping, without rest, a bassline so restless
& so long that it sound far when you beat it,
a bassline so perfect & correct that you feel
like you have to stand up and greet it,
so deep sounding like your hands could never reach it,
so far, so long. We had to let you go, had to
send you to meet it.

# FOR JOREL

That night she watch the door,
she watch she watch she watch
the hours of the door, her foot blinking
like a eye on the floor; she wait
she wait she wait, wasting
her time and her mind waiting
for this small boy she send to buy bread ever since,
waiting for this small bread of a boy
to come inside and be broken softly
under her hot hand of anger and love,
and the burn, the *blès* on his broad back of learnt lessons.
But all she could do that night is watch
the door like a *gwan nom* in front her,
all she could do was watch the time
increasing on the unopening silence,
all she could do was watch the clock,
make her son grow before his time,
making him come home so late
so late, so she wait, and she know
he must be on the road, playing
marbles and doing things things things
on the government road that he eh suppose
to do. "But the other boys was doing it too."
"But I don't care about the other boys, I care about
                    YOU!"
And all the talk she talk to herself, all the mop
she mope, she couldn't find no kind of comfort,
no explanation from clock,
and in the middle of her mind, she could see
a cock coming, a cock like a cop coming to her door,
with another day close up tight in it beak,
and before it could speak, she see herself start
lashing her thigh and she crow, "No! No! No!"
and the door turn to a mirror, and she walking

and he walking toward her, and she walking
and he walking toward her from inside the mirror,
and she inside the mirror too, but on the next side,
and they couldn't touch the boulder of each other
shoulder to roll away the reality.

Now she walking out the road,
with her curlers curl up nice on the bed
of her head, and she out in the jumping night
of her nighty, and her ol' slipper on her foot,
and she wishing she wishing she wishing
she could take it back, wishing the cock
could uncrow the day, wishing she could
take away the chores from his hands, take
back the poverty that feed children hunger
until they think they big big big, but they really big
with gas like imagination in their belly. But
she on the road now, woman alone, no man
to raise the boy, no high chest to brace against,
when the world has come, just she womanly on the road,
in the uncertain morning of midnight.

But he shoulda know to come home straight,
to not wait for no Tom, no Dick, no Harry,
to pass his ass home early so none of this
could happen; he should have come home
in the thick of his skin, smelling of *bouk* & ram-goat
as usual, with the piece of grass between his teeth
and bleat under her beating as usual; he should
have come home to cry and sleep and wake up
wiping the *lasi* from his eye, and say good morning,
with the sun in his eyebrows, and the world in his ears
and the trees and flowers in his nose;
he should have come home to where the tropical storm
of his mother love and lessons was brewing,

he should have know, he should have no

                                    no

                                            no

because dying was an adult thing
to do, something children should
be scolded for doing.

# SAMBO III

*The Least of his Brothers*

Uncle Bravely still comes
like he used to do on Sundays,
calling us, his brother's grandchildren,
"Uncle", looking from underneath
those barbed-wire eyebrows that
still prohibit his eyes; comes
again to the step of Sambo's well-
respected house. He doesn't ask for money,
or for rum. He does not even stick his tongue
to the side of his mouth like he used to, in
the way that made people call him *Woulo*.
He just comes – like the time when he went
out to sea and didn't return, when everybody
thought he had drowned – walking through his own absence,
wanting nothing more than to lift things, to feel again
the heaviness of life, then let go, to bob up and down
in memory like the cupped heart of a fishing boat
beating on the sea.

## SMALL ISLAND

To my Trinidad friends I speak like a good brochure;
I answer their picong about "small islands"
with my nostalgic backchat of country pastures,
my safe night-time beach strolls, the calm fireworks
of my island's colour. I tell them about how
our Indians are Negroes too, and Christian and safe
from the hot pimento of the Creole Trinidadian tongue.
I boast of homes that can breathe their doors peacefully open
into the night, that unlike Trinidad
violent crime clots predictably in the ghettos
where the victim is the murderer is the victim,
and the houses are too close to determine enemy
from friend, too close to need welcome mats. And it is easy
to talk like this staring out from South Quay to the horizon,
where my island is too far away to answer, stammering
with gunshots and the falling dead who can still be
named, singled out, and laid out carefully on pie-charts
or election speeches, or where pretty little crosses
and the soft vowel of a wreathe mark where some street legend
was knocked out of his name by the honk of a truck
coming round the bend. Everyone says a soft "*hisalòp!*"
in their heart and moves on. It never ends, but it is far
from this big oily island, where people slide easily
into stretchers everyday, belly-laugh their way out of breath,
lives wrapped in a roti of death.

## II

I am far away, at University, hitting the books,
*nyaming* doubles, going around getting somebody
child pregnant, eating roti with the hot spiteful pepper that
they call "mother-in-law". I call my mother in the morning
to tell her about the beautiful girl who is big-belly
for me, to worry her about the chances of me finishing
school. I call her at the time when she counts the dead
on the tele-obituaries and cries and says, "Poor *djab*", far
as she is from the ghettos, far as she is from Conway,
Marchand, New Village, Georgeville, Graveyard,
far as she is from Trinidad where her first grandchild
is being born in the undulating blood of this big island,
where every single day someone dies in country, suburb
or the city. The first love, and the last, is human pity.

# THE LIGHTS

The lights burn, and fit us
each into the moth-like mob
of shadows, beneath their blinding
bulbous light, brilliant like speech-
bubbles of God. All along the strip –
neons, fluorescents, street lamps lining
the street like mourners – each car
is a moving casket with a cortege trailing
them in the traffic. There is no one here,
only lights upon moving darknesses.
Their filaments have all burnt out
and all that is left, really, is the light.

The towel blooms
and withers, blooms
and withers in her hands,
as she wipes the last table
in the restaurant. An abandoned
cocktail grows water from its ice.
The smell & spillage & dirty dishes
linger like silent laughter
after the diners have left. Earlier, staff moved
about sunburned tourists,
order after order, in and out of the swinging
kitchen doors — a rhythm of service
that unsettled. I watch their
movements thicken with fatigue,
and no worksong, not even a *pitjay*
for them to sing. I want to show them my heart
softened with the moss of sympathy,
like a ruined wall at Pigeon Point.
So soon after. I want them
to hear the chains, the cutlery of empire
that I hear; to show them the deep history
of the tourist pocket. I finish what
is on my plate and think of how, once more,
I must walk the beach alone, gathering shells,
stones, the sea's coral-bones grumbling under
my feet, crunching and growing into a sedimentary
grudge, a gradual bucket of rage. She wipes
the last table — mine; her fingers splayed like roots.
I pick up my dread and walk.

# EBB II

I feel it when I am in the open lung
of my hammock, reading on the verandah
of my east coast apartment. I feel it
when I am driving down the Causeway
to Pigeon Island, with the sunroof pulled back,
letting the wind rough up my clothes.
Then I come to lie down on the beach,
to sit with legs crossed like a vendor's tray,
to settle and see the ocean and the true brochure-bright
colours of my island: the man selling fruits
on the sea, the fishing boats at Gros Islet,
the big-navel *ti nègs* running and diving
off the jetty with arms like huge tamarinds.
While I am there, a tourist smiles
a nothing-smile; a hotel worker fakes an accent
on the beach with flowers in his shirt whose roots
are killing his heart. Another man is offering horse-rides
and bright beach umbrellas. The pillars at the Sandals Hotel
separate the locals from the tourists.
I feel it when I take my toes out of this sand,
when I am leaving this place, when I am driving
on the Causeway, which feels, from inside my car,
as if it is made of breeze. I feel it when I pass
by my hammock and enter the small, aromatic alphabet
of the rooms in my apartment. I feel it in the cool dusk coming,
in the small ultimatums of light switches.
I feel it in the sound of the Atlantic entering the house, alone,
in the colourful silence of its precious stones.

# NOTES

p. 12. *Donbwé*: St. Lucian word for dumpling.
    *Djòt*: A St. Lucian stew.

p. 14. The "Educated names" in the poem, "Medium", are actually Vladimir, Nkrumah and Pablo.

p. 23. *Annafè*: see French *"en affaire"*. Rude and feisty.

p. 24. *Bullar/ boula*: a homosexual.
    *Nèg Mawon*: Maroon or, pejoratively, a wild Negro.

p. 25. *Gòjèt*: to hit or push someone on the throat.
    *Massa-day-done*: A phrase used to signify the end of colonial rule. "Master's day is done".

p. 26. *Mèg*: meagre, thin, emaciated.

p. 32. *Tjenbwa:* Obeah.
    *Malfini*: chicken hawk.

p. 34. *Kòkma*: see French *cauchemar*. A nightmare, or presser.

p. 35. *Gwan bwa*: forest.
    *Pawasòl Djab*: Devil's umbrella
    *Bwa Demou*: Devil's wood or bush. In the Caribbean, wood often refers to a stick, and has phallic overtones. See Dr. Zozo in Haiti or the meaning of Palo in Reglas de Congo in Cuba.

p. 36. *Devil's Bridge*: This refers to a Caribbean's Faust story. A man was said to have built a bridge in Morne Lezard in St. Lucia, with the help of the Devil, to whom he had promised the first "person" to cross the bridge. Instead, the man sent a dog across the bridge. Tricking the Devil, working a *jès* (jest).

p. 41. *Horn*: a verb referring to infidelity, to cuckold.

p. 48. *Zonbi*: a vagrant. Also used to refer to a lifeless body as well as a spirit e.g. *zonbi kouli* (an East Indian Spirit). See Zombie.
    *Mesi Bondyé*: Thank God. See French *"Merci bon Dieu"*.

p. 54. *Mwen Menm*: Me, myself/ You see me. Used to express mild disapproval.

p. 57. *Djouké*: to poke or to jab. Refers to a dance in which dancers jab their pelvic areas towards each other. *"Djouké sa"* *(literally* "jab that") is a dancing instruction given to the dancers to perform the action.

p. 58. *Djanmbélé*: onomatopoeia for the gyrating waist.

p. 60. *Sigawèt*: cigarette.

p. 61. *Blès*: internal injury; usually in reference to the chest and back area.
*Gwan nom*: Big man.

p. 62. *Lasi*: wax (e.g. in the waking eye).
*Bouk*: a bad smell. (literally "a billy goat")

p. 64. *Woulo*: a roll or spool.

p. 65. *Picong:* playful provocation; teasing.
*Hisalòp*: originally "ich salòp" (son of a bitch). This phrase was used in St. Lucia in the time of the guillotine. It was shouted as the guillotine landed and beheaded the convicted.

p. 66. *Nyam*: to eat.
*Poor djab*: literally "poor devil", but more accurately "poor thing"; an expression of sympathy.

p. 68. *Pitjay*: a work song sung while persons worked with a pickaxe.
*Nèg*: Negro; used pejoratively.

# ABOUT THE AUTHOR

Vladimir Lucien is a writer from St. Lucia. His work has been published in *The Caribbean Review of Books*, *Wasafiri*, *Small Axe*, the *PN Review*, *BIM*, *Caribbean Beat* and other journals, as well as in an anthology of poetry, *Beyond Sangre Grande*, edited by Cyril Dabydeen. Lucien was also awarded the first prize in the poetry category of the Small Axe prize 2013. He has been featured at the Bocas Lit Fest's new talent showcase as well as the West Indian Literature Conference, the Word Alive Literary Festival as well as other events. His artistic interests also include theatre, having acted and served as dramaturge in productions staged by the Department of Creative and Festival Arts, at his alma mater, the University of the West Indies (St. Augustine Campus). He is also the screenwriter of the documentary *The Merikins*, which premiered at the Trinidad and Tobago Film Festival in 2012.

# OTHER TITLES FROM ST LUCIA

Adrian Augier, *Navel String*
ISBN: 9781845232023 / 88pp. / £8.99 / Poetry

*Navel String* – complex, confident, always accessible – follows Adrian Augier's first work, *Bridge Maker*. This latest collection is powerful, the voice unfettered, even provocative, signalling conviction and confidence over both medium and message. Augier delves into issues of identity, equity, ownership and relevance against a background of irrevocable change in the physical and psychological landscape of St Lucia and the wider Caribbean.

Kendel Hippolyte, *Birthright*
ISBN: 9780948833939/ 120pp. / £8.99 / Poetry

*The Heinemann Book of Caribbean Poetry* described Kendel Hippolyte as 'perhaps the outstanding Caribbean poet of his generation'. He writes with satirical anger of an island marginalised by the international money markets in a prophetic voice whose ancestry is Blake, Whitman and Lawrence. These he marries to the contemporary influences of reggae, rastafarian word-play and a dread cosmology, with an acute control of formal structures and rhythm. *Birthright* collects all Hippolyte's earlier collections of poetry.

Kendel Hippolyte, *Night Vision*
ISBN: 9781845232351/ 80pp./ £8.99/ Poetry

Kendel Hippolyte speaks through and beyond tradition. He writes in sonnets and villanelles, in idiomatic dramatic monologues that capture the rhythms of Caribbean speech, in blues and rap poems, in free verse that draws upon the long-breath incantatory lines of Ginsberg and contracts in miniaturist forms as concise as graffiti. He draws upon all his verbal mastery and critical insight to draw sharp focus upon a nation in flux, where urbanisation expands and fragments his home of St Lucia. The poet turns his vision upon the people, the land and the culture, and finds a microcosm of the Caribbean in the 21st Century.

Kendel Hippolyte, *Fault Lines*
ISBN: 9781845231941 / 78pp. / £9.99 / Poetry

If you want to feel what it's like to live on a small island, vulnerable
to the wounded thrashings of world capitalism in crisis, where
livelihoods are destroyed at the flourish of a Brussels bureaucrat's
pen, where Paradise is a tourist cruise ship come to remind you of
your neo-colonial status, where global consumerism has poisoned
the ambitions of the young into drugs, crime and violence, then these
dread, urgent prophecies are indispensible guides.

Jane King, *Performance Anxiety*
ISBN: 9781845232306 / 122pp. / £8.99 / Poetry

"Jane King" is present but never obvious in these poems as the
observant eye taking in the beauties and droughts, climatic and
human, she sees in St Lucia and in the semi-public lives of her
neighbours. Hers is also the inward eye that plumbs dream states, the
unconscious and the alarming darkness that the free-floating imagi-
nation sometimes reaches. King is a distinctively original explorer of
the inner person, and of the world on the margins of perception.

John Robert Lee, *Elemental*
ISBN: 9781845230623 / 120pp. / £8.99 / Poetry

As Derek Walcott observes: "Robert Lee has been a scrupulous poet,
that's the biggest virtue that he has, and it's not a common virtue in
poets, to be scrupulous and modest in the best sense, not to over-
extend the range of the truth of his emotions, not to go for the
grandiose. He is a Christian poet obviously. You don't get in the
poetry anything that is, in a sense, preachy or self-advertising in terms
of its morality. He is a fine poet."

Earl G. Long, *Leaves in a River*
ISBN: 9781845230081/ 208pp. / £8.99 / Fiction

Long writes with unsentimental empathy about two people who are
desperate for fulfillment and choice, but who instead give way to

their impulses and pay for their decisions with an inevitability that Thomas Hardy would have seen as a truth of life. Long draws a vivid and inward portrait of a rural community with all its tensions between a desire for pleasure and a fearful sense of an all-seeing and judgmental God.

Garth St. Omer, *A Room on the Hill*
ISBN: 9781845230937 / 162pp. / £8.99 / Fiction

Attempting to overcome the guilt of a friend's suicide, John Lestrade retreats to a life of internal exile. Friends urge him to leave for education abroad, but he is discouraged by the cynical quest for personal advantage in the new anti-colonial politics amongst those who have pursued that option. The novel's astringent realism in questioning the direction of West Indian nationhood is finely balanced by its perception of untapped possibility.

Garth St. Omer , *Shades of Grey*
ISBN: 9781845230920 / 192pp. / £8.99 / Fiction

*Shades of Grey* comprises two short novels about young men, one separating from his past to pursue his own ambitions, the other trying to construct his own story. First published in 1968, *The Listener* called it "one of the most genuinely daring and accomplished works of fiction ... for a very long time", whilst Kenneth Ramchand wrote that St Omer's "delicacy, control and economy must surely place him in the first rank of twentieth-century novelists."

Garth St. Omer, *Nor Any Country*
ISBN: 9781845232139 / 124pp. / £8.99 / Fiction

Peter Breville returns briefly to St Lucia en route to a university post elsewhere. After eight years away in higher education, he discovers a country that is on the point of change, but where the economic and cultural disparities between the new middle class and the impoverished black majority is no less wide. In the midst of this, he must decide what he owes his wife, Phyllis, who is waiting loyally for him, but with whom he hasn't communicated in all this time.

Jean Antoine-Dunne, Ed. *Interlocking Basins of a Globe: Essays on Derek Walcott*
ISBN: 9781845232207/ 224pp. / £16.99 / Literary Criticism

These essays range from discussion of Walcott's earliest poetry in *Twenty-Five Poems* (1948) to his most recent collections that explore encroaching old age, *The Prodigal* (2004) and *White Egrets* (2010). The contributors to this collection are predominantly, but not wholly, Caribbean-based, which ensures that, whilst his position as poet of the world is celebrated, the roots of Derek Walcott's writing in the Caribbean is the central focus.

All available online at peepaltreepress.com
or email orders to orders@peepaltreepress.com
or phone +44 113 245 1703